Amalfi's
of
Chandler

"Our Story"

GIUSEPPE & SERGIO MIELE

i

Dedication

This book is dedicated to all the Fathers and Mothers involved in this industry. When it comes to the work force, the restaurant business has never changed. Whether you're a cook, dishwasher, or a server, you will always be the essence of the industry.

Thank you.

Table of Contents

Preface

You may ask, "Why are we writing this book?" It's not about teaching you how to open your own business, how to deal with people, or how to get rich in our industry.

We are just sharing our experiences, ups and downs, stories, and the different types of people we have encountered in our "never ending adventure." The number one reason for us to do this, was that every time we were with friends and family, someone always asked us, "How's work going?" The answer was always, "You know, one day busy another day slow," and "You know what happened?" Then we would explain about something funny or silly that had happened.

Now, it didn't matter how many people we told our stories to, they all had the same answer: "Wow, you guys should write a book!" And there you have it. We hope that you enjoy it!

Grazie, Giuseppe & Sergio

Background

In 1978 my brother Giuseppe, at the age of 17, moved to New York City from Naples, Italy. He spoke little English, he had little money, but he had lots of courage and determination. After a short stay at our aunt's house in Long Island, he decided it was time to move on. He rented a room in a house in Whitestone, Queens and got a job at a local Italian restaurant. I could say that was the beginning of a journey in the restaurant industry, but I would be wrong. You see, both Giuseppe and I grew up in a coffee shop owned by our father, located in Naples, Italy.

Dad's name was Antonio Miele. He was very charismatic and well-liked by people. Unfortunately for my mom, he was also very popular with the ladies. She had to keep him in line all the time, but that's a different story. Anyway, we learned a lot of things work-related that shaped who we are today, and we have to thank dad for all his patience.

He was often harsh in the way he treated us. It was no easy task to deal with work and family at the same time. Nevertheless, he expected us to work better and harder than any other employees. He used to say, "If you don't care, they don't care. So it was clear that we were in for long hours of work.

Giuseppe was in charge of daily deliveries. Let me explain how deliveries were done back then. First, there was no car or any other means of transportation other that your feet.

Second, a heavy metal tray was your tool. Customers from the neighborhood, such as the butcher shop, barber shop and so forth, would call on a daily basis and place orders for espressos, cappuccinos, drinks, pastries, etc. Basically everything we sold. Once the order was placed, Giuseppe would load up his tray with coffee mugs, spoons, napkins, and go deliver. Once he arrived at his destination, he would greet everybody, and start setting up for service.

This wasn't your typical, "Here's your stuff and have a good day," it wasn't that easy. That's because now he had to earn his tip. He would start conversation with a little local gossip, then he would say they were always his first stop, then throw some jokes in and did whatever he could to make them feel priority number one. A lot of work went into it. You have to consider not all the customers were likable people. Once they finished what they ordered, Giuseppe had to bring all that was used back to the shop, all of this time knowing that there were other customers waiting. Most importantly, he had to prove his efficiency and his better capability compared to the other employees.

By the way, in all of this, you have to understand that he was only 11 years old! Do you get it? Only 11 years old! So you have to entertain, deliver the goods, be likable, polite, fast, and think like an adult. Not to mention that if somebody said something wrong, Giuseppe would put them in their place. Dad would immediately receive a phone call from the customer saying his son acted in a rude way. When he got back to the shop, after dodging all the scugnizzi (street bullies), he had to listen to Dad complaining about him and receive punishment. This was an 11 year old boy, working for what today would be a 50 cent tip! As I'm writing, I don't understand how people (customers) would act in such ways.

Forward to our business today. You see that while we now have computers and use cars for delivery or place orders online, the clients haven't changed a bit. They are always priority number one.

It doesn't matter what happens, the client comes before anything else. If the power goes out in my restaurant, guess what? It's my fault. If the weather is cloudy, guess what, it's my fault. If the TV is on the wrong channel, once again it's my fault. And this is when Dad comes into play. All those days and hours spent at work, all the punishment and etiquette of work that were instilled in us. That made us excellent at what we do, even when the power goes out. Grazie, papa. (Thank you, Dad).

Now let's talk about me a little bit. I was also born and raised in Naples, Italy. But it was a bit different for me. By the time I started working with my dad, we no longer offered deliveries, so my learning experience happened inside the coffee shop. The bad thing about it was that my dad had his eyes on me all the time. He was always telling me don't do this, don't say that. Man what a pain in the neck. I started memorizing the customer's habits. This person drinks espresso in a short glass rather than your typical coffee cup, another guy would drink cappuccino with no foam, and yes ma'am your hot chocolate was made with hot water as usual.

You are starting to see that I was learning all the basics without even knowing it.

At the age of 12 I felt I wanted to try and work for someone else. When I told my dad, he never said anything about it, but I'm sure he was impressed with my decision. It took a while and I found a job in a coffee shop in the city's amusement park.

In the beginning I worked weekends from 8 am to midnight, with a 2 hour lunch break, with the pay being $12 a day. Yes, it was lousy pay, but I was gaining a lot of experience. At age 14, I was put in charge of a kiosk. I sold soft drinks, ice cream, coffee, candy, and pastry. The pay was a little better, and being in charge felt very good. I was proud and always thinking about work. Today I have applied those experiences to my own business. Part of my staff training today includes making business decisions. I want my employees to feel proud and care as much as I do.

Going back to me at the age of 18, I joined the Italian Navy. After a few years I was bored and left. I had a little money saved and I started traveling. I spent time in Spain, France, and Greece. Once back home a friend offered me a job in an Italian restaurant in Germany. I accepted it immediately, and that was an adventure, considering that I was only 21. As I was getting ready for my trip, I received a call from Giuseppe, who was living in New York. When I told him about my plans, he asked why Germany, when I could come to New York and stay with him. He didn't have to say it twice. I packed my stuff and "arrivederci Italy."

So, seen through the eyes of a 21 year old immigrant, New York looked magical. All the smells, the colors, and the people, it felt unreal. I still remember the first hot dog bought from a street vendor in Flushing, Queens. In the beginning I had a hard time adjusting. I didn't speak English and I had no friends. I got a job in a pizza shop and I immediately knew I was born to do that. As challenging as it was, I enjoyed the entire package;

dealing with the customers every day, doing the orders, prepping the food, you can never get bored. Don't get me wrong, it's a lot of work, but don't forget where I came from. It's like as if my father knew what I was going to do all along. So all the time spent under his watchful eyes came in really handy. Even in my broken English, I would take better care of the customers than my English speaking coworkers. It's funny, people would call to place an order and they'd ask for me. It was nice to know, and I felt ready to open my own pizza shop.

So there it was in 1995. We opened up Fortunato's Pizzeria in Bethpage, Long Island. After a few years, the partnership with my brother wasn't going well. To make matters worse, there was very little money. Giuseppe walked away and got a job in Brooklyn. A little later, I also walked away, and got a job in Queens with a friend. A few years went by and I had adjusted to my life in Queens. Giuseppe called me and told me he decided to move to Arizona. I was happy for him, but at the same time, I felt sad to know we were going to be far apart.

But life goes on. In the meantime, I fell in love with a girl I knew from our neighborhood in Naples. Little did I know that we were going to get married. We started a long distance relationship. It was hard, because we spent a lot of time apart from each other. But in the end it all worked out. Now the big question was, "Do we move back to Italy or do we stay in New York?"

The decision was up in the air, so we took a trip to Arizona to see Giuseppe and his family. In my heart, I was sure I was going to move back to Italy. But, I wanted to say good bye. Little did I know how beautiful Arizona could be? I decided to move there. We developed a plan to open up a pizzeria. Since my wife was waiting for her green card, she was back in Italy.

Both Giuseppe and I got multiple jobs and saved every penny. Three years later we opened Miele's Pizzeria located in Tempe, Arizona. I remember we put everything we had into it. The shop was ready, and everything was in place. The food, drinks, licenses, permits, and a few helpers. Also with that came a lot of fear. We had no backup plans and we only had $250 in the business account. We managed to stay open, because after the first year, we started getting busy. That felt good. During that period, we won numerous awards and we were also featured in the local news.

I liked my job, as it was our place, and we made a living out of it. Our next step was to change from a pizza shop to a full service restaurant. So we started adding more entrees, pastas, and Italian specialties. Things looked pretty good. And then the recession happened. Week after week we saw customers losing their homes, their jobs, and moving away. Businesses were shutting down all around and it went on that way for a while. We opened up, got customers, then the recession hit and we lost customers. You have to reinvent yourself all over again. Try that when you only make enough money to get out of a hole. But, we did it! Thank you Dad once again, for he was present in our minds.

All he had taught us came together. We lifted ourselves up, changed the menu, and paid attention to the customers wanted more than ever. We listened, listened some more, and changed. You know what?

We did well, and we also expanded to a second location, bigger and better. And that's Amalfi Pizzeria.

Success

It is a big word that requires a lot of respect. Nevertheless, in 2005, we decided to challenge that word. And boy oh boy what a challenge it was. Thinking that we knew everything about the business, we quickly realized there was way more to be learned.

We did what we thought was enough research on what we thought it took to be a success in the restaurant business. We took all of our experiences from our past, including Miele's, as well as from a number of people that had some form of success in their own business. What we found out was that a lot of businesses, not just the restaurant businesses, had some of the same characteristics as we had in the past, but also a number of different ones.

So we kept asking a number of people who were successful in their own business for their recipe. We came to find out that the differences were amazing such as their backgrounds, their experiences both good and bad, as well as where they had found advice for their start-ups. It appeared to us that there were some basic ground rules that you had to follow, but not the same recipe worked for everyone in every type of business.

Opening of Miele's

As most of us know with any business, it normally takes more time than what you might estimate to get things done and working smoothly. No matter how well you plan, even though we had experience before doing things and working, things were different this time. Location, types of customers (age & income), getting servers, kitchen help etc. all played heavily in our endeavor.

Once we opened Miele's Bistro things were going along fine. It was there in front of our eyes. Good food, great atmosphere, and a reliable staff to back us up.

There were also various awards to top it all off. We felt as though we were really independent and on our own. The problem with our initial success was that it also brought on negative items that we never really thought of when we decided on our adventure into the restaurant business. It became a roller-coaster of emotions having to balance between work and family.

Time at Work

We spent a lot more time at work than we did with our wives and children. We always try to thank them for their support and understanding. But, there is always trouble lurking out there where you least expect it.

It is not how much you know that hurts you, it is how much you don't know that hurts you. When we think back at our careers, as well as others, you spend more of your waking hours with people at work, than your wife or kids.

Think about it, at home or elsewhere, too many times issues come up that need your attention, but you are not there to provide support or to fix them. Kids grow up, we grow older, and really do not think about how much time we are away because of being "at work." And in our case, it was normally at a restaurant.

If you look at 24 hours in a day, in your normal workweek, we spend:

- 10 hours at work
- 7 hours sleeping
- 7 hours with family (maybe)

Out of a 24 hour period. About 70%of your day is away from your family and loved ones. This causes issues that you know about, and more importantly may not know about.

The Silent Killer

*"It starts slowly and you don't even realize it is happening. The days, months and years go by, and you die inside a little more. Inside you feel abandoned, disconnected and numb. Your kids don't know their dad and they're sad. Why? Because their dad is a restaurant owner. It sucks up so much of his time and he can't be there. He misses birthday parties, school plays, meet the teacher night, conferences, dances, and football games. He was not around to witness first words, first steps, and first foods. There was no time. He had to be at the restaurant or, as I would call it, the **family wrecking** place. It is a place that kills dreams and happiness.*

It is a place that our kids wished never existed. The place that stole their dad.

You will never get that precious time back. You disconnect with the man you love.

How, you ask? Due to the lack of time to make memories, with the most important people in your life, is how it happens. When he had time off, it wasn't any quality time because the stress and exhaustion owning a restaurant endures. The interruptions by a phone call. A call that said that someone did not show up for work or the AC died.

The stress of the bills being paid, the stress of wondering if your employees will show up. You are depending on strangers to do the right thing just by showing up to work. You deal with everyone else's problems, but you don't realize you're creating your own. I feel bad for the person I once loved, because he was too overwhelmed to love me back.

I used to think it was me, but I don't think so anymore. I think all the stress of owning a restaurant ruined him. It slowly killed his spirit and to witness that was tragic.

He tried to do the right thing by financially taking care of us, but not being there physically or emotionally, wasn't worth all the money in the world. I didn't care if he was successful, I didn't ask for much, I just wanted to be happy. I dreamed of a happy family and wanted to laugh. At the end of the day, when he walked in the door there was no happiness, just defeat and disappointment. I couldn't stand the stories of customers complaining anymore. I was your biggest customer and I hardly ever complained.

So the next time you want to send a dish back because you didn't know what you were ordering and didn't like it, think about it for a minute. Whose fault is it? The time you want to complain about having to pay extra for extra sauce, or the time you ripped the person I love apart on the Internet, know you did not only hurt the owner but you hurt his family as well.

When you are at a family owned restaurant, understand the amount of hours it takes to run that business and the hours that the dads cannot do their jobs at home. Try to be appreciative and realize a lot of sacrifices come to owning a restaurant. The biggest being the loss of a connection to the owner's family. This is why I call this the Silent Killer." (A wife's point of view)

5

Taking Care of and Dealing with the Customer

This is definitely no easy task. It is not just about smiling, serving food, and cracking jokes. You have to realize that even when you have done your best, you could have done a lot better.

Customers can be very demanding in our current location. The reason being that there are a large number of retirees and near retirees. Being located in the southeast valley of the Phoenix area, the climate normally attracts these types of people from all over the US.

Owning an Italian restaurant in this area automatically brought comparisons of our restaurant to those back home. A lot of our customers are from the Midwest and the East coast. Some of our customers can sometimes be critical in regards to the menu, our house wine, and the types of table cloths that we have on the tables.

The comparison is made between all of these items and what they were used to seeing "back home." In all fairness to the customers, we have made some improvements based on some of the constructive criticism from our customers. Many times you think that you have things working perfectly from an owner's viewpoint, but from the customer's side it is quite different.

What we try to do is listen and then make a determination if something really needs to be changed for the better. Customers love to see their ideas implemented as it makes them think that they are part of the business, which they really are.

$1 Worth of Meat Sauce

It's a beautiful Sunday. I get up, hit the shower, and get ready for some breakfast with the wife and kids. My wife had made a tasty apricot crostata, which translated means apricot tart. My kids and I were just indulging ourselves in it. Once I was done, I kissed them goodbye, and went to work. I had already made a mental list of all the prep work that was to be done. Around 9:15 am I walked through the doors of the restaurant, my brother Giuseppe was already there, finishing up with all the paperwork of the week.

The coffee was ready, so I grabbed a cup of it, and sat at the table with Giuseppe. I asked him, "What's up?" He said "Nothing much, I'm just trying to make sure we have everything we need for the day and hopefully it will be a busy Sunday." He also informed me that one of the refrigerators was not working properly, so he had to empty it out, and unplug it. I then placed a call to our repair guy and made sure that he would come on a Monday versus Sunday, thus avoiding paying double for the service. There is one thing you must know, when operating a restaurant: Saturdays and Sundays are like holidays, everybody wants to get paid double.

Anyway, around 10:30 am, the rest of the crew came in. While I was slicing mushrooms, I kept an eye on the pizza dough that was rapidly mixing. My cook was mixing meatballs, and at the same time, he was giving Giuseppe a list of produce he needed for the day. The sign "open" was turned on at 11 am, and like usual, people started coming in. By 11:45am the smell of baking meatballs had taken over the restaurant. There was an old couple that walked in. Giuseppe said "buongiorno" to them and sat them at a booth. They looked like two birds in love. I looked at them and they looked back at me. The lady had a big smile on her face and the gentleman wanted to let me know that the place smelled really good. I guess it was the power of the meatballs.

Shortly after that a family of four came in. It was a husband and wife with two kids. They were seated and the waitress gave them menus. Then she started to explain about all the daily lunch specials. In the meantime, Giuseppe was going around the room making sure that everything was in order. I was baking bread and the day looked pretty good. At one point the waitress came into the kitchen and informed me that a customer had a request. It was the gentleman with wife and kids. We will call him Jay. Jay wanted to know if he could add meat sauce to our meat lasagna instead of the marinara sauce that usually comes with it. I told her to tell him there was no problem and I would have been glad to substitute the sauce and that there was an "up charge" of $2 for the meat sauce.

The waitress went to the table and went on to explain about the $2 "up charge." Next thing I know, Jay stood up in the middle of the room complaining about the $2, and wanted to know, what was the "up charge" for? He approached the kitchen counter and started arguing with me about the $2. Needless to say all eyes were on me. I explained to Jay that meat sauce was extra because of the meat that goes into it. And that's why there was an "up charge." Still he was not happy about it. So I told him, "Don't get the meat sauce," because the lasagna had meat in it anyway.

And, he would have enjoyed it, even with the marinara sauce that came with it.

But no, he felt he was right and started to raise his voice. At that point I could see that his wife and kids felt very uncomfortable. Even the cute old couple told Jay to shut up and sit down. Out of the corner of my eyes, I also noted Giuseppe was going towards Jay. Once there, he again explained the meat sauce was extra and that is all there was to it, very simple. So Jay looked at me and said, "Ok, give me a dollar's worth of meat sauce!" Now for me that was it. I told him, "Why don't you try and get a dollar's worth of French fries at a fast food restaurant and see what they would answer." I then asked him to leave the restaurant and to please never come back again.

He told me that he would never come back, that our food was horrible, and we were going to go out of business very soon. Once he was gone we all looked at each other for an explanation. We were stunned by this person who clearly had no idea of his own doing. We resumed our work and the rest of the day was good as usual. At the end of the night we all went home. As I was on the highway driving back home, I started thinking about this Jay person. I mean, why would a person act in such way mistreating the waitress and myself? I have done nothing wrong, and as all these thoughts are crossing my mind while driving back home, I never realized how fast I was going.

So now I'm getting pulled over for speeding. I tried to explain to the police officer that I had a long day at work, I was tired, and apologized for my speeding. The officer sympathized with me but he said that was no excuse for my speeding. Therefore, at the end of the day, I now have a speeding ticket. I got home and you can imagine how furious I was at what happened. Jay insulted me at work and because of him I even got a speeding ticket. Once I walked into the house, I saw my wife in bed reading a book. She looked at me with a smile and asked me how my day was. I wanted to tell my wife about what happened, but I also knew that the story of my day at that moment, would have come out very badly. So I simply shrugged my shoulders, I kissed her and said, "Good as usual".

Then I went to check up on my two little angels; they were asleep as usual. I say as usual, because I very rarely get to see them before bedtime due to my work hours. But when I see them, everything changes. It's like a light switch. All the daily problems are left behind and all that matters are my two little angels. Monday comes rolling in. My wife is getting the kids ready for school, I get my cup of coffee on the go, I drop off my kids at school, and I'm on my way to work. At 11 AM the repairman is coming in to fix the fridge. I'm hoping for an inexpensive fix. I'm the first one in the restaurant and a few minutes later one of the cooks walks in, as well as one waitress from the day before.

Everything was getting set up, and as I was chopping potatoes and carrots for a special soup of the night, the waitress tells me, "Hey, do you remember the guy from yesterday?" She was talking about "meat sauce Jay." I said, "Yeah what about him?" She says, "He wants to talk to you on the phone." I told her to hang up the phone. I didn't want to talk to him. She says, "Well actually he's here." I looked to my left and saw him standing by the front counter. I'm sure that at that moment my face looked like it was going to explode. How could he have the courage to step into my restaurant again?

I'm thinking this is not good. Is he here to insult me again or to tell me that he's going to put me out of business? Whatever was the case, I thought that this wasn't going to be good, so I glanced at him and told him I'll be right there. As I was walking towards him my thoughts were, "Should I throw him out, or should I call the cops?" I was getting frustrated by his presence. I walked around the counter and asked how I could help him.

He told me that he wanted to apologize for his behavior. I stopped him right there and walked outside with him. I didn't want him to feel uncomfortable since my staff was there. He began to tell me how sorry he was and that he understood he was completely out of line. He said his family loved our food, and he wanted to be able to take his family to our restaurant. I was shocked. Here I am ready for a fight and Jay is there apologizing to me. I told him I was happy about his apology, but I needed to discuss his request with my brother, after all he is my partner.

Jay asked me if he could talk to Giuseppe in person, and I told him he would be at the restaurant at 3 pm. Sure enough, they met at 3 PM, and Giuseppe accepted Jay's apology as well. To this day we still don't know why on that Sunday things escalated in such a way. All we know is that Jay is now a great customer. He comes by with his family very often and sometimes he just stops by to say "Hi." We want to share this story with you because it was for us, a learning experience. It does not matter how you react if it happens to you. I just wanted you to know that I was ready to rumble out of frustration and it would have been a terrible mistake. You must have heard the saying, "Don't judge a book by its cover?" I did, and yet with all my experience, I was so close to making a fool out of myself. Lesson learned.

You have to also understand that you can't possibly please everyone. A prime example is that a customer once told me that my lasagna did not taste like his grandmother's lasagna. At that point my answer was, "I would love to meet her one day so that I could learn from her." What was going on in my mind was that, "Of course it doesn't taste like your grandmother's lasagna, because your grandmother doesn't work here!"

Another time a gentleman walked in and ordered a bruschetta. Keep in mind that the menu described the bruschetta as follows. Toasted slices of bread, with fresh tomatoes, garlic, olive oil, and basil. After eating it he said that it was just bread with tomatoes. So I thought to myself, which part of bruschetta didn't you understand? It has always been a classic; bread, tomatoes, and garlic. In the end, it has always been our fault, even when the customer doesn't know what he is eating.

Acceptance of Customer's Comments

The sooner that you understand this situation, the sooner that you will be able to accept this experience. It may be common and you will learn how to serve your customers better.

One thing that we learned early in our restaurant business, is that if a person or a group likes your restaurant, they will tell someone else of their experience. But, if the person or group has a bad experience, they will tell 10 people. It does not take very long to have a couple hundred people know that someone may have had a bad or terrible experience at Amalfi's!

Now as far as we were concerned, this was a fact a few years ago. But today everyone has "social media" to express their pleasure or more importantly displeasure. Think about it, we go out for dinner, have a great time, and then go home. Opposite of that fact, we go out for dinner, have a bad experience for whatever the reason, we go home, get on the computer and tell the world of our experience. Or even better yet, as we are waiting on our menu, drink, appetizer, or entrée, we are on a cell phone telling everyone that we know on Facebook what a lousy experience we are having.

Full Room

Friday nights are normally a full house for us. Twenty-three tables are taken and there is only one left. A couple comes in and gets seated at the last table. They order a glass of wine and iced tea, along with one 10 inch individual pizza. Nine minutes later they are complaining about the wait. When you walk into a restaurant, and you are seated at the last table, it may be an indication that your pie will not be out in the next 5 minutes.

Another thing that we had to think about and customers should try to understand is where you will be waiting if the restaurant is full. Many restaurants have a large seating area while you wait. Our building that we occupy does not have that physical arrangement. This is especially true if we have a lot of carry out orders, like happens so many times on Thursday through Sunday evenings. Some restaurants have seating outside and use that space for the "overflow" of customers waiting.

Another thing that we have to understand as well as customers is that a full house may or may not accommodate your favorite seating that you have been accustomed to previously. A lot of our customers want to have their backs to a wall so that they can see everyone coming and going without turning around.

On Friday and Saturday nights especially, we may or may not be able to accommodate customers with that request. But what we can do is try to have them wait a few minutes for their favorite table or at least a specific seating area. Based on the information that we have in the area where we are currently located, we know about what time each day of each week that most of our customers tend to show up. Using this information we have been able to tell a few of our customers that if they really want a specific seating area, that there might be a better time to come for their meal.

Using the technology that is available today allows us to gather a lot of information on how to address a full room when and if it happens. Some customers appreciate us trying to meet their needs even though we a have a full room, others have not.

Mr. Big Bully Jim

Since we only have 23 tables, it's not a huge restaurant. So, during crunch time, it fills up very quickly. At times, it seems like everybody gathers outside, and then they all come in at once. Imagine this; the phones are ringing off the hook and approximately 80 people sit at the same time. They are all hungry, thirsty, and in a hurry to catch a movie. That's not a problem for us, we have learned from our past mistakes, and we know how to deal with it.

There's always a solution to the problem, so you make adjustments, and everything works out well. For example, we have a policy in place where we don't accept reservations for parties of two. That's because most of our tables are set up for four people. If we had 10 reservations of 2 it means that 10 of our tables are not at a maximum profit. Obviously those tables are going to create a small check. Yes, don't forget that in the end, we are still running a business, with expenses such as rent, insurance, employees, licenses, and all kinds of fees. But in the midst of all that, we are still able to serve good food at a great price, and in a friendly family atmosphere.

I now present to you Mr. Big Bully Jim and you must listen to this. It's Friday afternoon, Giuseppe is restocking the bar, as we are all getting ready for a busy night. The phone rings, Giuseppe answers it, and it's a Mr. Jim requesting a reservation for 2 people at 5:30 PM on that evening. Giuseppe explained that we don't take reservations for 2. He also went on to reassure Mr. Big Bully Jim that there would be plenty of tables available at 5:30 so no need to worry about it. Mr. Big Bully Jim replied by saying it was B.S. and he wanted a reservation at 5:30 pm for 2 people. Now, Mr. Big Bully Jim is becoming vulgar and a bully over the phone. But you know what, again and again we have had this experience, and Giuseppe politely repeated, no reservations for 2 are taken at this restaurant.

Mr. Big Bully Jim's last words over the phone were, "We'll see about that!" Giuseppe and I had a big laugh about it. We were under the impression that Mr. Big Bully Jim, was bored with his life, to the point of entertaining himself by acting like an arrogant bully on the phone. Out of nowhere that Friday evening, we were packed at 5 pm. Now, we are aware of the fact that some of our good customers come in pairs, so we always have few tables for 2 ready. We also know Mr. Big Bully Jim, has promised us he would be there at 5:30 pm, and we are not about to find ourselves in the wrong situation.

It's now 5:24 PM. There were about a dozen people standing up waiting for their tables. Some of them were drinking, some of them were talking about what they were going to eat, and others were just checking their cell phones. I was directing the kitchen like a fine tuned machine. My crew was perfect. It is in the busiest moments when we operate at the best. Giuseppe was chatting with some of our regulars about the dinner specials and that's when it happened.

Mr. Big Bully Jim stormed in, moved in front of everybody, and demanded to speak with Giuseppe. Giuseppe asked, "What can I do for you sir?" He answered, "My name is Jim and I requested

17

a table for 2 at 5:30 PM. Now because of you, look at this, I have to wait." He was being very aggressive and rude. All of the people standing there had a questioning look on their faces, as they were probably thinking what's wrong with this guy? Giuseppe told Mr. Big Bully Jim, that it was 5:24 PM and assured him in front of everybody that if we didn't have his table ready at 5:30 PM, we would "comp" the entire dinner, including beverages, and desserts.

Keep in mind that Mr. Big Bully Jim was so busy being a bully, he never noticed the 2 tables available, and all set up ready to go. That's because we are not going to look unprofessional. We know what we are doing and based on the earlier phone call by Mr. Big Bully Jim, we were expecting him. Mr. Big Bully Jim started pointing his finger towards Giuseppe and he began insulting him. At this point, even some of the guests who were already seated started to listen.

It was happening in front of them (talk about dinner and a show it only happens at Amalfi Pizzeria!). You now know the customer is always right, but when the customer (he or she) is insulting my brother, me or my staff, you are definitely not welcome in our restaurant. I don't care who you are, or how much money you have. You could be a doctor, a pilot, or a prime minister, as it makes no difference to us. I want you to know that if you are an insulting bully, we will waste no time showing you the way out. That's what happened to Mr. Big Bully Jim.

Television

Early on, we had to determine what kind of restaurant we wanted to be. We decided that with our background and experience that we did not want to be a "Sports Bar" type of restaurant. Whenever we went to a sports bar, it was extremely hard to listen to the person next you to you, much less someone seated across from you.

What happens when you have TVs is that you run into the situation of, "I want to watch the football game, he wants to watch baseball, and she wants to watch the food channel." Give us a break. What happened to spending quality time over dinner, enjoying good food, and the company that you are with? And while you are at it, turn off the cell phones!

The Customer is Always Right

The customer may not always be right, but they will always be the customer. The customer has many functions in your business. First and foremost they pay the bills, provide free advertisement (both positive and negative), and ultimately determine how long you will be in business.

On many occasions, actually most of them, we can prove to the customer that he/she was probably wrong. But, in doing so, it is going to make it a worse situation. You will always run into someone who watches the food channel and thinks of herself/himself as a chef. When that happens, I dismiss them with a smile and a "Thank You" for letting me know their thoughts.

Once a lady asked me for a plate of pasta al dente. After the meal was served she complained that the pasta was frozen because it was hard. Al dente pasta *means* undercooked pasta which means the pasta will be a bit harder. Again, a "thank you very much" was in order.

How much Wine?

I remember when we owned Miele's pizzeria it was a lot of fun. We had a mixed variety of clientele. Many of them were from New York and New Jersey. You know them, it's easy to pinpoint them. They are loud and always have a fast answer. You either love them or hate them. In our case, after spending many years in New York, it was very easy to love them. They're not bad, they're just very opinionated. There was this lady that used to come there with her boyfriend. They ordered the same items all the time, it was Caesars salad for two, fried zucchini, chicken Toscano, and baked ziti pasta. Glass of Pinot Grigio for her and a beer for him, and all was good. They always enjoyed our food and always complimented us for making them feel at home when dining there.

At one point the server was accommodating another party of 4. Being that Miele's was a small restaurant, with just 13 tables and 8 seats at the bar, it was very easy for Giuseppe and me to keep eyes on all tables. So, I felt I should go see if everything was good as usual with my customers. I made sure they all had bread, oil and vinegar, and asked if they needed anything. The gentleman asked for a beer and the lady wanted another glass of Pinot Grigio. I told them I'd be back with their drinks.

Before I had the chance to walk away from the table, she told me to make sure that the glass of wine would be filled to the top, because the previous one was not the proper amount. Now, we give a minimum of 6 ounces at all times for a glass of wine. And trust me, all of my servers give even more than

6 ounces, because it's not coming out of their pockets, and that's fine with us. It makes the customer feel good and that we are taking care of them. So when she said that about the glass of wine, it seemed very strange to me. I called the server and asked him about the wine. He told me he had poured 6 ounces of Pinot Grigio and he used a fancy wine glass, basically a bigger one.

So, I took it upon myself to show my good customer that I was not about to skimp on wine. I poured the 6 ounces in the regular small glass so that it was full to the top. I then put it on the table. She was very pleased and loudly said, "Now that's a glass of wine." I then picked up the full glass of wine and emptied it into the bigger glass. She realized that it was always the same amount of wine, just a different glass. I also explained to her that we were switching to bigger glasses, to let the wine breathe better. This was like asking what's heavier, a pound of lead or a pound of feathers. A pound is a pound no matter what. But, when it comes to the food and beverage industry, would I use that example with my customers? Well that's entirely up to you.

I am still in business and I now own Amalfi Pizzeria, with my brother Giuseppe. Different location, larger location, same good food, and many new customers. But you always encounter the same questions like the wine amount. This is the nature of the business. Like the New Yorkers, you either love it or hate it. This is our experience and we keep on learning, thanks to you.

Happy People

In the past 20 years we have dedicated our holidays and weekends to this industry. And being very serious, it just burns us up when we see people sitting at a table with a grumpy face. Rather than being thankful to be able to afford a night out, having the time to do it, they just sit there, and take it all for granted. Not to mention the people that bring their own problems into the restaurant and expect you to do something about it. We keep thinking that maybe they forgot to take their medication. Sorry, but not our fault. Your husband did not buy you flowers; sorry, but that probably was not our fault either. The waiter/waitress is too short, too tall, too old, and too young, too anything that may not be our fault either.

We think that people have to remember that you come into a restaurant to eat, not to be analyzed, and correct a few of your own issues. Problem solvers we are not, we may just look like ones.

What we do try to provide is a dining experience that will accommodate any type of attitude that comes through the front door. I know that we just said that we are not analysts, or trying to fix a certain behavior, but in many ways we are like a barber. When a guy goes to the barber shop, they sometimes ask for or give an opinion to their barber. In turn they may or may not want a reply or an opinion back.

Same way in a restaurant. The severs may or may not be questioned for an opinion if you know the server well. In our restaurant, we are small enough that we can interact with a number of customers one on one, depending how busy we are.

Servers: Pros and Cons

In our careers, we must have seen just about 250 servers. They come in all shapes and sizes, races, and gender. Good or bad, most have one thing in common, "How much can I make?"

My answer is, "As much as you want." A food server should take that into consideration when given a table. The more he/she sells, the more he/she pleases the customer, the better the chance, I repeat, a chance, of a better tip.

The pros are:
- Of waiters/waitresses, we have been very fortunate to have had a great crew
- Though a few bad apples show up every now and then.

The cons are:
- They all seem to get sick the same weekend
- Their cars all break down at the same time (are they in a car pool?)
- They all have a sick pet
- They all do not have a working alarm clock
- The most unbelievable is that when they come to work, they are all texting, on Facebook, or playing games on their phones
- But when I call them, there always seems to be a problem with their phones
- The most frequent answer is a low battery, my phone was on the silent mode, or I must have left it in my car

- Don't you just love technology?

Suggestions

Once again everyone is a "restaurateur." It usually starts with a customer telling you that you should have a larger bar, why don't you sell Italian ice, your furniture should be more romantic, you need more candles on your tables, you should deliver, you should have more of a selection of salads on the menu, the straws should be longer, and every other detail that anyone might imagine.

We could write a book on all you need to.... Oh, wait a minute that is what we are trying to do. What people do not realize is that everything in a restaurant has, for the most part, already been designed, tested and approved by people who do this for a living.

As an example, maybe your landlord doesn't allow you to make deliveries for insurance purposes. Maybe there are no candles on the table because you have customers with children and they can get hurt. What we are trying to say to all the people that give us this type of advice is, "How about you laying out $350,000 to open your own restaurant?" Then, we will come to visit to see how you are doing, given the fact that your money is on the line.

Partnership

If you look at a traditional partnership it could be defined as:

"A single business where two or more people share ownership. Each partner contributes to all aspects of the business, including money, property, labor or skill. In return, each partner shares in the profits and losses of the business. Because partnerships entail more than one person in the decision-making process, it's important to discuss a wide variety of issues up front and develop a legal partnership agreement.

This agreement should document how future business decisions will be made, including how the partners will divide profits, resolve disputes, change ownership (bring in new partners or buy out current partners) and how to dissolve the partnership. Although partnership agreements are not legally required, they are strongly recommended and it is considered extremely risky to operate without one."

That was fine for all of the lawyers and accountants, but we are not lawyers or accounts. We are brothers. And for us we had a different definition.

For us a partnership is an easy concept, normally wonderful in the beginning. It will take a few weeks to realize that you want to kick, choke, beat, and run over your wonderful partner. This is coming from brothers who are partners. Having a partner is much more difficult than you think. A stranger or a friend can be dismissed a whole lot easier than a brother. Worse things can happen as you may lose a friend or worse, money.

In our case being brothers as partners for the past 20 years, we have gone through some tough ups and downs, fights, and disagreements. But nevertheless, what has saved us was a common goal. It is that you must support the family!

The best thing about our partnership is how different we are in the way we eat, speak, dress, and even our taste for cars, etc. We think that this is part of our success. When it comes to a new dish to be offered, when one of us doesn't like it, we can usually work it out. Both of us can compromise to be able to offer something suitable for our customers.

Even though many years have gone by, we are still learning from one another, and it is still a great ride.

Fresh out of the Oven vs Ready to Go Pizza

People make this comparison all of the time. No matter how long a pizza has been sitting, without being eaten, it is available for a lot of people. They like the availability of it just being there with no waiting! After spending 12 years in New York, the #1 question of most customers picking up a pizza is, "How long has that pizza been sitting there?" It has always been about a fresh product with us. Today, thanks to franchising, doing it only for a quick profit, you have it ready in a box and you know nothing about the pizza. Maybe we are old fashioned, or maybe times have changed, regardless it seems to be a shame to us.

Customers frequently tell us that pizza must come right out of the oven with exactly the same ingredients that they ordered over the phone or while they ordered it right in front of us and waited on it.

I guess that we can understand that some people really do not care where the pizza came from, or how long it has been there under the heat lamp. Many are just hungry, don't have a minute to waste, and need either one slice of this or a slice of this and a slice of that. That just isn't our business, never has been, never will be.

We understand that we can't be all things to all people, but we have to have the understanding that one piece of pizza may be all that is required to satisfy someone's hunger. But since we are in the restaurant business our offering is a pizza in many sizes with just about any ingredient that you want for your toppings.

Décor

As the saying goes, "back in the day," it seems like all that was required for your restaurant was a bench, a couple of chairs, a mirror and nice looking Italian flag and you had a pizza joint.

Today, forget about that. Go check your review on "Yelp." They will start out with:

"The walls were painted beautiful."

"Oh my gosh, the chandelier was beautiful."

"The table was set very gracefully."

"The floor was like a mirror."

"And lastly, the ambience was lovely."

Forget about the food. The people are out doing site inspections without looking at the menu. Give them a view on the patio and they will be extremely happy with just about anything including popcorn. We are trying to figure out what happened to, "This food is tasting amazing!"

Sometimes we feel that every customer that comes in is a food critic hired by the local newspaper to analyze the interior of the building that we occupy. Or they could be a building inspector looking for violations in the internal structure so that no one gets hurt.

We have been in business long enough to know that people become critics if they know what they are talking about or even if they don't know what they are talking about. Sometimes people are feeling that they are being helpful if they give us tips on the drapes, the blinds, light fixtures, etc.

After all, how could 2 Italian guys ever figure out how to decorate anything, even the bathrooms?

Cheese vs Pregnancy

A couple of days ago I was prepping the line for our general customers that would soon be coming in. A young couple came in and approached the bar. The young lady was pregnant. As they were looking at our menu and what we had to offer, she asks the question of one of the waiters, if the mozzarella cheese that we used was pasteurized? So the server comes in the back where I was prepping and asked the question regarding the type of cheese that we used. Of course I know that it is pasteurized because we have been using the same type of mozzarella cheese for the past 20 years. I told the server to tell her not to be worried, that it was pasteurized and no harm would come to her child. However, he told the young lady that there were no problems or issues with our cheese.

I remembered that my wife had expressed the same concern when she was pregnant with our children, So, I decided to go out and make her feel a little more comfortable. Before I answered her question, I walked back into the store room and brought out the cheese that we use on our pizza. She wanted to know that her child who would be coming into the world would not be harmed. I showed her that it was pasteurized cheese that we would be using on her pizza. I showed her the label on the cheese to ensure that she was comfortable ordering a pizza with this cheese on it. She then gave me a smile like thank you so much for having an interest in the welfare of my new child about to be born. She said that being pregnant, everything was against her and working against her first born child. But, it was great that someone like me was taking an interest in her as well as her child's welfare. Then she said that she would like to order a "Margherita" pizza. I said fine, but I advised her that we use a different type of cheese on a "Margherita" pizza.

I didn't know if she would know the difference in the two cheeses. So, I went to the back room to get the fresh mozzarella cheese that we would be using on the Margherita pizza. I brought the block of cheese back out to show her it is a different kind of cheese, also pasteurized but not exactly the same as the first block of cheese that I showed her. She started laughing and was talking to other customers about how nice it was for someone to take the time to explain the difference in the chesses to a customer. She was super, super happy with the experience. After they received their pizza, I am sure that they left happy and I thought maybe I had a new customer just based on that experience. To me, this type of experience and effort is sometimes hard to find.

The reason being, a lot of managers and even owners of a restaurant will not take the time to explain to the customers what goes on a certain dish being ordered and served. To me it makes a difference. I know that all of franchise restaurants and even family owned restaurants talk about customer service, but how many of their customers really leave with a smile on their face knowing that someone really took the time to explain the ingredients, much less the origin of the ingredients.

The next time that you order a pizza, no matter if a franchised restaurant or family owned, ask them about the cheese that they are using. You might be surprised at the answer(s) that you may receive.

And Then There is Yelp

Like many other inventions, Yelp is one of those wonderful ideas that is supposed to help consumers and businesses. Consumers can access information regarding products, services and other things through Yelp based on other people's comments and reviews.

On the other hand businesses can improve the way of doing things by adjusting in accordance with a customer's request if and when possible. With that in mind, Yelp can be a great tool, but in the wrong hands it becomes a weapon against businesses because it is easy to hide behind a computer screen and write all sorts of things that are not true.

First, understand that because my brother and I are in business to earn a living, we want to establish a relationship with customers where he or she keeps coming back. All comments by the customers are always taken in consideration because without the customers we won't be in business.

In one of the latest reviews, a customer says, "I went to Amalfi Pizzeria and while having dinner I noticed that the owners weren't there. Shouldn't they be there?" According to this person we have to be there anytime and all the time 24/7. But that is their opinion. I guess we're not allowed to have an emergency, we cannot attend a birthday, we cannot be stuck in traffic or we cannot be with our family right?

I don't get it. I have been banking with Chase for 15 years. I have both a business and a personal account. After 15 years I haven't met Mr. Chase or whoever owns the bank. Yet I have to be in my restaurant 24/7? Give us a break.

There are always going to be bad reviews and good reviews. The point is, when it comes to restaurants, if you say "no" to a special request, or if the table the customer wants is taken by someone else, it'll just set off a bad review and when they're mad about one thing they're going to try and bring the house down.

So it starts like this. The server says, "Sorry that table won't be available for another 20 minutes." The customer gets mad due to us not being able to perform a miracle, such as having a table appear from nowhere.

Naturally, as soon as they go home they get on Yelp and here it comes, the review: "I can't believe I was charged extra when I asked for extra meat, the place was too dark, the server wasn't paying enough attention, it took 1 minute and 39 seconds to get the drinks, I didn't like the color of the napkin, the parking lot was too busy and blah, blah, blah."

So we become the punching bag and we are picked apart only because you had to pay for the extra meat. Imagine this: you go to a gas station and buy $20 worth of gas. After paying, you then ask for a little extra gas free of charge. Does that make sense to you? If not, it's because you must pay for the extra gas. Now let's see if you are going to do a write up on Yelp about having to pay for extra gas.

Once again, if you don't get the extra for free it's a big deal. Our opinion about reviews is that when it comes to our decision on buying something or going somewhere, we no longer look at reviews.

Whether it's Yelp or any other online site, we find them misleading.

We feel, due to our own experience, that there are always 2 sides to the story and, when it comes to reviews, you only see one side - the customer's.

For any information about a product or a place we always ask friends or family for their opinion, and surely not a stranger online. Yelp, good or bad? The decision is up to you.

Epilogue

By Jim Villella - Author of *Creating and Maintaining Success*. Amazon.com 2016

First of all I am not a food critic. But I have been in and eaten in a number of restaurants and military mess halls in the US and other countries in my last (60) years. Some bad, some good, some great. I think what makes the difference in a good to great restaurant is the following one word.

Consistency.....

Even though this is only one word, it is the hardest concept to attain in any business, restaurant or any other. A great restaurant will:
- Have a server that is attentive to your needs
- Have a menu that accommodates most people's needs. This does not mean that an Italian restaurant will have (4) types of hamburgers
- Accept reservations
- Accommodate customers with "special needs"
- Accommodate "gluten free" selections
- Have a greeter that welcomes you like they are glad to see you
- Have servers that know their menu by heart
- Provide your order in a timely manner. This would include scheduling your drink, appetizer, and entrée at the right time so that

you can enjoy your appetizer with your drink, prior to the entrée showing up
- Have restrooms that are clean, clean, clean
- Have ample parking
- Have a "happy hour" menu
- Provide "specials that may be offered at a reduced price
- Have exterior seating, weather permitting
- Have a full-stocked bar including an array of wines and beer on tap
- Have several TVs for sports lovers, as well as a good array of wines and beer on tap
- Have competitive pricing
- Have a great chef. Serve only food he/she can brilliantly create. (and another #1)
- Obtain knowledgeable, pleasant, helpful, courteous and friendly staff from host to servers. They must like their job and show it
- Have food that must be good, fresh, and attractively presented or no one will try it again
- Have a menu that must offer great choices but need not be overly extensive. The best restaurants have limited offerings
- Determine beforehand what type of restaurant you are; American, steak, vegetarian, ethnic, etc. You cannot be everything to everyone

- Offer a dessert tray to show. It cannot be fake. The best are actual desserts that can be served as chosen
- Have a good descriptive oral menu or printed menu

If your favorite restaurant can accommodate the above bulleted items, you have the makings of a "Great Restaurant."

If you think this looks like a "Wish List" it is. But I challenge you. The next time you go to your favorite restaurant, see how many of these items you can "check off" to see how many they can meet. You may be surprised.

I would like to go back to the "greeter" for a moment. The greeter is the 1st person that you normally meet when you enter a restaurant. This person, in many instances, can be very young and somewhat limited in experience. My personal opinion is that the greeter represents the eating establishment and should be a top level manager or owner if possible. I know that this is not always possible as many restaurant owners like to start new employees out as a greeter, then promote to server, and then on up within the restaurant's organization.

Now back to Amalfi's Restaurant. My wife and I first started going to Amalfi's back in January or February of 2012. As soon as we walked in, we were greeted by Joe. Since then, whenever we go back, we are almost always greeted by Joe a majority of the time. He will also call you by your first name if you have been there more than a few times.

During this time, I have seen a number of servers, both men and women come and go just about like every other restaurant in the southeast valley. But, for some reason, when we see a new face there, they seem to have a good grasp of the menu, are attentive, and treat you like you are their only customer.

Joe and Sergio have not only found the right recipe for their food, but also for bringing in new personnel who quickly perform their duties like seasoned veterans. One other item, the majority of the time I eat there, I order the same thing, Parmigiana Seafood Fra' Diavolo. This is shrimp, calamari and clams in hot spicy marinara sauce. Always the same, how can I complain?

Again, Consistency.......

www.ingramcontent.com/pod-product-compliance
Lightning Source LLC
Chambersburg PA
CBHW070409190526
45169CB00003B/1184